"To the attentive eye, each moment of the year has its own beauty, and in the same field, it beholds, every hour, a picture which was never seen before, and which shall never be seen again."

—RALPH WALDO EMERSON

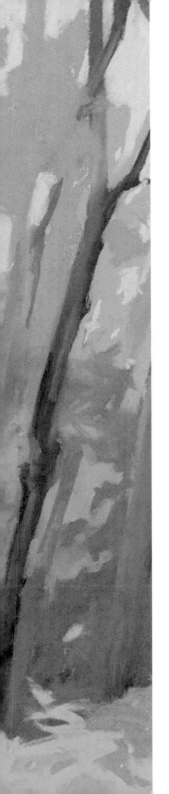

Nature and Design

The Landscape Moderated and Guided

by Alexia Scott, MFA

Left Image: *Walk in the Fall, Great Falls National Park*, pastel 24 in. x 36 in.

Nature and Design
The Landscape Moderated and Guided
Written and Illustrated
by Alexia Scott, MFA

Green Pigment Publications
Falls Church, Virginia

ISBN: 978-0-0015547-6-8

Contact: Alexia Scott
AJ@Alexiapaints.com
www.alexiascott.com

Artwork and Photography: Alexia Scott
Book Design: Marinda Scott
Editor: Linda Scott

Right Image: *California Valley, Big Sur,* pastel 14 x 14

This introduction to the basics of design and the landscape will use examples in three media: Pastel, Oil Paint, and Acrylic Gouache. It depends on what I am painting, which I choose, but the design is always relevant. What an artist paints, not the medium, is unique to each artist.

Cover Image: *Silver Lake Aspen, June Lake, California,* gouache 12 in. x 12 in.

"Being creative, doing something lasting to share with others, is a rewarding adventure!" —ALEXIA

In this small square, I have tried to use at least one third of the space for the bold flowers. It is important to think of the whole space not just the subject.

Morning Glories, pastel 5 in. x 5 in.

Table of Contents

Left Image: *Mount Palomar and Spring Snow*, Oil on Canvas, 36 in. x 36 in.

Before you begin to paint, you need to
think about design.

Before you explore color, you need to
think about design.

Before you draw a line, you need to
think about design.

What is Design

Design is the deliberate process of arranging artistic elements to create a cohesive picture. This is what makes a viewer look at one painting and not another.

Design is the natural visual language of art. If I place a horizon line on a blank horizontal canvas and draw an object like a simple chair near the horizon, it usually implies restful. If the chair is large and partly extends past the edges of the painting, you will think of it as congested. If it is above the horizon, it appears light of weight, and if it is tiny and low toward the left, you might think of lost and lonely.

Could you visualize these statements without an illustration? Most of you can because you already understand the language. Advertisers and illustrators have been showing it to you all your life, and it is just as valuable for you as a landscape painter. You might think the landscape is out there in the field and I paint what I see or the garden is there and I pick a section and paint it, but you do look around at different angles, levels, and zoom in or out. This is a good start.

What you need to ponder first is what caught your attention. The first thing you saw and made you want to paint the view must be your primary goal. If you start there and make all of your painting choices reflect this first impression, your painting has a much greater chance of success. Don't get bogged down in the details.

You have an elaborate arsenal of tools at your disposal to make your painting speak to the viewer. You can change all the classic placement ideas by changing the light or color to lead the viewer's attention to where you want it. The continually evolving view before you offers hundreds of choices; shadows move, clouds pass over, and the sun travels across the sky.

One of your first choices should be the size and shape of your painting. This choice should be based on your painting mood: vertical - active, horizontal — restful, square — intimate, and equal between you and the viewer. Refrain from always using standard sizes. Don't let the art supply manufacturers dictate your artistic intentions. If you are working on paper, give yourself more paper to allow for adjustments as you conceptualize. If you are working on canvas, you can tape it to a board and stretch it later. If you are working on a panel, you can fix plenty of evil designs with a saw. The important thing to realize is that it's not right. This seems to be an intuitive action; most of my students know when something is not working. Listen to your instincts; they are usually correct.

Bixby Bridge, Big Sur, California, oil on panel 24 in. x 24 in.

Bixby Bridge is a perfect example of allowing the sun to help you design. We had been over the bridge several times at all times of the day. Early one morning, heading south on California Route 1, there it was, the painting I wanted to paint. I think you will see this in your own search for landscapes; you will know it when you see it. The visual language of design is in your mind; if it wasn't, none of the design's visual devices used by advertisers for capturing your attention would work. They are speaking a language you already know, but you do need to understand what you know.

STUDIO HISTORY OF DESIGN AND THE LANDSCAPE

From a studio artist's perspective, even though we understand this language of design, it was a long time before we utilized it to its most significant potential.

Early Christian fresco painters were illustrating scripture because much of the population were illiterate. The artists would often use gold leaf to catch your eye. The Italian artist Masaccio was one of the first painters to use linear-perspective to direct the viewers' eyes to the nails in Christ's feet in his fresco painting of the Trinity around 1427 in Florence. No one in Europe was paintings landscapes for the sake of painting a beautiful view and natural space. In 1565, the Dutch artist Pieter Brueghel The Elder painted a sequence of landscape paintings called Months of the Year. *Hunters In The Snow* by Brueghel is a large oil painting on a wooden panel that is part of this group that clearly expresses the use of the landscape to capture the viewer's attention. The artist's use of contrast within the stark snowy landscape is a favorite to all who study landscape painting and design. By the 1600s, Italian artists were focused on using dramatic lighting or chiaroscuro to tell their stories. This style of painting is called tenebrism.

Back with the Dutch in the 1660s and 1670s, we see landscapes by artists Jacob Van Ruisdael and Aelbert Cuyp. The Dutch are an entrepreneurial people, which tells the other Europeans that there is a market for landscape painting. We now have this new genre, but it will be about a hundred more years before they catch on.

On the other side of the globe, the Chinese are making ink landscape paintings centuries earlier. Their calligraphic writing style—characters drawn with a special brush—enhanced the scholar's dexterity as they practiced writing; they also practiced painting. The painters meditated, looking across a landscape allowing their thoughts to follow the hills and streams, and then painted a version of what they wanted to remember and share with others. Landscape painting in China was considered their highest form of painting. While in Europe, the historical narrative paintings were considered the most significant subject for painting.

THE 19TH CENTURY

Artists, although independent personalities, still live in the world and are influenced by a time and place. By the time the Revolutionary war began in 1776, it had been 170 years since the British colony of Jamestown was settled in 1606. In the wilderness of the young United States, a group of artists, Thomas Cole, Asher B. Durand, Frederic Church, Albert Bierstadt, and others, would become known as the Hudson River School. Each, in their own way, studied the land, geology, and atmosphere. They sketched on location outdoors to understand the landscape, the form of the trees, and the receding space. In their studios near the mouth of the Hudson River, they created enormous canvases of the inspiring landscape.

In the truest sense, landscape painting as a genre began in the 19th Century. The Hudson River School coincides with R.W. Emerson, the transcendentalist movement in New England, and his essay "Nature" in 1837. These artists saw nature as grand, wild, and omnipotent.

Sparrow at The Daily News, Carlsbad, California, oil 6 in. x 6 in.

This little Sparrow sat above my head on a wall under an awning. All the design elements were there, just not in the best places. Diagonals on a square picture, just like the bridge and shadow in Bixby Bridge, keep you grounded within the square formate and lead your eye across the painting. However, diagonals are active elements, suggesting the Sparrow is about to bolt!

In England, the 19th Century brought us William Turner and John Constable. They painted the gentle English countryside and created atmospheric impressions of the sea.

As an understanding of visual language, design seems to begin here in the 19th Century for the landscape painters when the western artists were introduced to Eastern philosophies. They added another essential tool to their ability to communicate.

The mid-19th Century found Japan emerging from a two-century isolation. In 1858, trade reopened and artistic exchange of ideas and processes began a new. During Japan's isolation, the Italians discovered Linear Perspective, and in Japan, artist Hokusai produced his landscape prints, Thirty-six Views of Mount Fuji. The Japanese style of design brought a new structure and use of color to European artists. Having seen some of the prints, the French impressionist embraced the Eastern artists' use of space within the picture plane. The influence of Japonisme in Europe filtered in through not only painting and porcelain but teaching as well. Hokusai Manga was a teaching manual for Hokusai's students and was published in 1814 but didn't reach Europe until after the end of the Japanese seclusion. It is easy enough to observe Hokusai's influence in structuring the picture plane and use of color by studying the French Impressionists, especially post Impressionists such as Van Gogh, Cezanne, Gauguin, and Bonnard. By following the trail of some of the educators, you can see how ideas move from one continent to the other. Art Critics and historians don't necessarily focus on the same concepts that the artists

strive to achieve. One such educator is Arthur Wesley Dow from Ipswich, Massachusetts. Dow lived in Paris to study art between 1880 to 1888, where he was introduced to woodblock prints of landscapes from Japan and papers on the artistic process.

You cannot teach art unless you make art. AW Dow studied in France for 8 years and found himself drawn to the colors and structure of the Japanese style. Japonisme was very popular, and some might say, trendy today; however, it never ceased to influence our artistic timeline. Dow returned to the young United States with its new schools, ideas, and unique landscapes. In 1899, he published his book, Composition: A Series of Exercises in Art Structure for the Use of Students and Teachers. His books became the textbooks in many of our public schools. Dow felt that our Nation's high school students should study and understand art. Art textbooks from the 1920s include his book on composition and are still available. Unlike other art education platforms, Dow realized these ideas on design applied to all creative forms: where other educators created a separation between painting and woodworking, he did not.

Are you beginning to realize that there are many paths to follow in picture-making? As you explore, look at the percentages of the spaces and color forms. There is no right or wrong, no book you didn't read; your only rock in your path is not working on painting. This path to painting is yours, and the more you are exposed to the process, the more tools you will have to be creative.

Evening, Jackson, Wyoming, pastel 10 in. x 20 in.

The Aspen Dance, Nevada,
oil on panel 16 in. x 20 in.

The beauty of nature and
landscape painting is the
freedom you have to manage
your space. When possible, I try
to start on location. I can make
important decisions regarding
space and percentages of
values I plan to explore from the
view in front of me. I was only
able to do a sketch this time,
but I realized what reference
information I would need for the
painting through the drawing.
If you have no other choice but
to work from your photographs,
please take ten or twenty. Take
at least one photo further
away, several where you like
the composition, and several
up close. The camera wants
to keep everything in focus,
but you don't. The camera is a
help, but has limitations. Your
memory is your best tool for
working off-site. When you are
back in the studio, the memory
of why you wanted to paint the
view will have deleted the most
unnecessary elements.

Tracks in the Snow, November,
oil on linen 18 in. x 28 in.

Tracks in the Snow began with a gesture drawing in raw sienna; not with fancy ink painting strokes but sloppy, brushy swishes of diluted oil paint. I wanted to share the sudden brightness of the setting sun that November evening. Nothing lasts very long at that time of day. The clusters of dark objects surrounding the bright sun helped to increase the glow.

This is a critical time in any painting; finding your way and setting up your structure will give you the skeleton of the design you need to move forward.

Values become shapes within the painting design. Establishing the dark area and how much of a dark space is necessary to feature the setting sun is intuition. There is a long-held rule about thirds; however, it seemed to need more of a two-thirds percentage of the canvas to heighten the bright sunlight.

Balancing the light with the dark as the sun went down didn't give me much time to explore different possibilities, which was helpful in this case. I didn't have time to lose what I loved about the view. This view is from my rearview side mirror as I pull into my driveway. Remember to take a lot of photos for reference, but rely on your memory.

Tracks in the Snow, November, oil on linen 18 in. x 28 in.

Now that your painting has its basic design, you need to answer the question: How far do I want to go with this painting? You should always work from abstract to detail, never detail first. It is difficult at times to hold on to your design throughout your painting process. In time, it will become easier to listen to your instincts. Things will pop out to you because they are visually "out of place". Don't leave them; fix them!

THE 20TH CENTURY

Georgia O'Keeffe studied with Arthur Dow at Columbia University's Teachers College in 1914. It is fair to suggest that she was also exposed to Dow's textbook on Composition much earlier during her secondary education in Sun Prairie, Wisconsin. Like most of us, she had many teachers. Each teacher adds something to your style and vision. Each naturalist and landscape artist she enjoyed studying added to the ideas she expressed on her canvas. She brought about a new American Modernism in the landscape where design is the important subject.

Nearly all American landscape artists emerging during the 20th Century benefited from art education in high school and a good foundation in the principles of design. This process led to design movements in the secondary arts as well. Through the design of a flower, nature draws the bee to the pollen at times by ultraviolet colors only seen by the bee. You can draw the viewer to your landscape design by understanding how the configuration of elements, color, shape, and value relates to your picture plane's space. Artists tackle this in many ways, but when your instincts tell you something is out of place, it probably is. Trust yourself.

Toward Evening,
Anza-Borrego Desert, CA,
oil on panel 16 in. x 20 in.
This began as a study of the rocks but ended up a color study as the afternoon light warmed on the desert.

The Elements of Design

Breaking down the puzzle of design is best tackled by starting your painting with one element and subordinating the rest.

The elements of art and design are line, shape/form, color, space, value and texture.

LINE

Vermont Field in August, oil on panel 11 in. x 14 in.

Driving across Vermont a few summers ago, following the Connecticut River as much as possible, we came across a farmer plowing his field just after a sudden rain. The colors were vivid and the air clear, but it was the lines the tractor and farmer made in the earth that made me stop to watch.

There really is nothing lovelier than sunlight; unless it is afternoon warm sunlight which is almost intoxicating. Therefore, sunlight plays a big part in this theatrical performance on my panel, but still, the focus is on the lines.

The line directs your eyes but also closes to make shapes.

SPACE

Over the Edge, Big Sur, pastel 12 in. x 18 in.

I wanted to use the space of the picture plane to suggest this cliff as a high drop-off. I didn't really want to stand any closer, and I thought the congestion of the space created a little tension. I could have suggested more cliffs and the water below, but that is the usual picture. The space of your picture plane is up to you to control the shape, height, and width. Using standard size is easier to frame but less creative, and you forgo an essential tool.

You want to use all your tools to create your art, and one of the most important tools is the shape of your canvas, paper, or panel.

COLOR

White Mountain Near Carmel by the Sea, pastel 24 in. x 24 in.

Leaving the sea behind and driving into the mountains east of Carmel, you will find more beautiful landscapes. California colors are soft, with the tan grasses providing contrast between the natural wildflowers and spring greens. In Virginia, all things are green by May. Changing the greens as I receded the space gives more depth to the landscape.

Controlling the color is your job. Warm colors come forward, cool colors recede.

VALUE

The El Tovar in the Fog, Grand Canyon, oil on linen 22 in. x 28 in.

One April trip to the Grand Canyon, I couldn't see the canyon. The clouds filled up the void like marshmallows. Along the rim, the foliage marked our path, and close-up elements were evidence that the rules of atmospheric perspective were obvious to all.

Color has value: Close objects have a full value range from light to dark, and each movement back in space diminishes this range of value; mid-ground has half the value range as the foreground; and the background has a minimal range with no detail.

SHAPE/FORM

The Blue Bunting, Shenandoah NP, Oil on Linen 50 in. x 64 in.

I enjoy painting large natures-scapes; they help me feel like I am in the woods or garden while in the studio. However, they are hard to control because they are created, not copied. There are many shapes of leaves, flowers, and the shapes formed by the spaces between them. There is also an overall form to several clusters of flowers, stems, and leaves. The trees in the background also create a dark form as they visually unify as a dark shape.

All landscape elements are based on your basic shapes of spheres, cubes, cylinders, and cones. Try not to lose sight of this concept because light always shines the same on a cylinder as on a tree trunk.

TEXTURE

Road to Julian, California, oil on canvas 54 in. x 54 in.

Texture in the landscape can be foliage, a melody of flowers in the foreground, or distant trees growing on a smooth plane. It can also be clusters of detail in a setting of open space. I have never deliberately created a painting that I would consider "texture", or my main reason for painting it, but it often becomes part of the structure as I work.

Look for texture in your landscape as a tool to describe and control the environment you are painting.

Cape Ann Sand, Massachusetts, pastel 5 in. x 5 in.

Pastels provide both surface texture and image texture. I often travel with pastels, and this small study was made when we visited Cape Ann, just north of Boston. I was focused on the color, the sky, and the brush. Then why did I make so much sand? It just seemed to work; it pushed me right up into the color.

Exercises: PASTEL, GOUACHE AND OIL PAINTING

Stone Bridge Blue Bells, Bull Run National Park, pastel 12 in. x 24 in.

I'm not sure how many paintings I have painted of our Virginia Bluebells, but they are such a treat each spring. This painting focuses on the edge between the distant Bluebells and trees emerging from winter; the rest of the pastel is just suggestive.

I find it creative to switch from one painting media to another depending on what I am painting. When traveling, I take pastels or acrylic gouache. With pastels, you choose colors, and at times, you must be creative because you have a limited range of colors. With gouache, you are mixing colors and I handle them just like oil paint; however, they dry very fast. The Japanese used water-based media in both printmaking and painting. Each media has its advantages and disadvantages. Design and the structure of placement doesn't depend on a particular media because it is about space, color, relationships, and harmony.

All media have advantages and disadvantages, but switching between these three will keep you learning. I hope to show you that design is essential and that the media you use and the way you handle it is yours to explore.

PASTEL

Supplies:

- Sanded Uart 400 paper. My paper is 18 in. x 24 in. but you can use any you have handy.
- Earth-tone pastels; you will need a variety of colors, choose any brand you like. Note: You can't mix oil pastels with regular pastels.

Give yourself a nice set of colors; don't try to match mine. Do your own thing and have fun!

As you look at the supply list for pastels, gouache, and oil paint, I hope you will notice the difference in the amount of "stuff" you need when painting. Pastels are the easiest to work with. You can sit and paint with just paper, a drawing board, a box of Prismacolor 96 Nepastel, and a towel. I use my fingers to blend!

Remember, we are working on composition!

I started this pastel by deciding on a horizontal or vertical painting; even though the mountain touched the sky, I wanted the remnants of the snow dotted through the landscape. I began drawing the edge between the sky and the land; I needed to decide how much sky, mountain, and water to fit into the picture plane. Should I pull back or close-in on my view? I want you to see how loose and undefined the painting started. Don't be heavy-handed with your pastels; allow room for exploration.

Certainly no detail yet, but I did want to suggest the snow; it made for such a nice contrast and texture with the rocks and dirt. I am drawn to the warm earth tone of the sunlit peak. This is a time when the color is important to me.

Add in the suggestion of the green trees and grasses as just zig-zags in place. Some blue on the shadows reflective of the sunny day. These are all colors put in place but no detail.

Notice how the greens and blues are smudged, and the trees begin to form by drawing the ground color and snow to silhouette their shape. I work all over the painting, never completely defining an area yet but laying down colors to suggest the form of the mountain.

I want to make sure you realize how expressive you can be with pastels. These green marks are far from carefully made, rather mere suggestions of granite in this volcanic landscape.

Adding to the darks helps establish the composition (note: I use the terms composition and design interchangeably). As I meander around the pastel marks, I realize I have been avoiding the foreground, and that yellow-green is not really working.

Adding more detail and arranging the snow patterns. I now need to work on the water and the foreground.

Give the snow a little more form by edging it with the ground color. Don't make all your shapes by drawing the shape. Try to draw your shape by drawing the color of the surface the shape it is next to. This gives you two chances to control that shape. Shapes are everything.

High Country, Yosemite, June 2021, pastel 18 in. x 24 in.

Just a suggestion of still water at the mountain base frames the mountains adding depth, texture, and repetition of color.

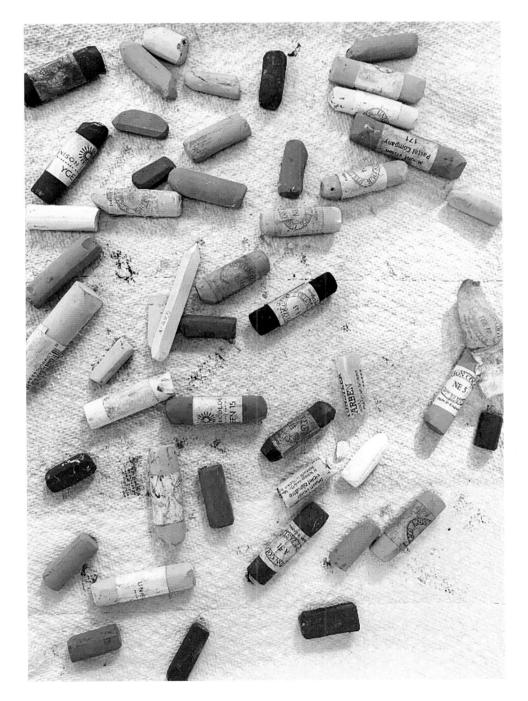

This is the collection of pastels I used for *High Country*. All three media require you to keep track of your colors. If you don't, and you throw an oddity into the mix, it will cause inconsistency rather than harmony. As you use your pastels, lay them on a separate tray and look around your painting to find additional places to use the color.

This is an iPhone X image. Your artwork will always look different in a different light. If you paint outside in sunlight, the light in your home will cause you to lose some of the colors you have so carefully chosen.

I realized I missed that yellow-green; here it is again. It was easy to find the color because I had the tray of colors separate from my many, many pastels. Sometimes your first instants are worth paying attention to.

It's Snowing, Great Basin, Nevada, pastel 8 in. x 8 in.

Comparing these two 8-inch square snow paintings should show you that the brush strokes are very similar between the pastel and the gouache painting. The square end of the pastel provides a flat mark and a thin line by using the corner. The flat brush is the same—flat stroke or line by using the edge of the paintbrush. Oil painting also handles the same with a brush, just not the same brush.

GOUACHE

Above Twin Lakes, Tamarack Lodge, California, gouache 8 in. x 8 in.

Snow is a favorite subject of mine, not sure why but I always want to paint it. The snow provides excellent contrast and reflects subtle colors. All three mediums allow for manipulation of the picture composition while you are working. I prefer to just start painting and refine as I go along. This is why I want you to think of design first when you begin to paint. Never, never start with detail.

Carson Peak, Silver Lake, California, acrylic gouache on panel 8 in. x 8 in.

During a recent trip to the June Lake area, I brought small panels and acrylic gouache. Oil painting is what I do the most, but it is hard to travel with by air. I handled the gouache precisely as I do oil paints, using a limited palette. Painting en plein air, the light changed, clouds went by, and the sun moved. To focus on design while in the field, try to establish your percentage of dark and light and the focus you want for the painting. With acrylic gouache, pastels, and oil paint, you have some flexibility to paint the way you want, something you only saw for a moment but wanted to paint.

Cicadas 2021, Falls Church, gouache 5 in. x 5 in.

It is hard to design when bugs crawl up your legs, so I finished this in the studio. I wanted to focus on the cicadas and their shadows. Acrylic gouache is opaque and you can paint on top of what you have already painted, correcting your composition. You don't want to start tight.

Acrylic Gouache Supplies:

- Holbein artist's acrylic gouache in Yellow, Ultramarine Blue, Pure Red, Sap Green, Violet, Crimson, Olive, Raw Umber, and Raw Sienna.

- 10" x 10" panel, or whatever you want to paint on

- A container of water

- **Masterson Sta-Wet Palette:** Gouache dries so quickly and this palette will help you to be able to use your color mixtures until you finish your painting. This will help those students that are new to mixing paint. I use this frequently when painting outside with acrylic gouache.

One afternoon, we visited the old stone bridge over Bull Run in the National Park. We usually visit in the spring but this was an August visit, and the wildflowers were shoulder high. While wandering, I spied a group of adult praying mantis on the yellow aster flowers. Their bodies matched the shape of the leaves, and they were well camouflaged. I began this study by painting the leaves close to me because I wanted the mantis to be life-size.

I worked on a white panel this time and placed splotches of yellow for the flowers in a natural arrangement and where they would look best within the composition of the painting. Early in the painting, I placed the mantises.

There are two mantises and darker yellow for petals under the bright yellow flowers, which help the mantises with their camouflage.

Next, I began to work into the spaces behind the plants: distant trees and cooler blue to work some of the leaves into. If this was an oil painting, I would have toned the canvas first, but I was worried about the yellow flowers losing their bright hue with a toned canvas for this painting.

Spending time on the foliage in the lower half helps stabilize the design of the painting. I am not sure yet about how much of the painting I want dark. I am trying to place the mantises in a proper environment. I want the first glimpse you see to be the yellow flowers.

Most of the panel is covered, and I like the blue for the distance space. The mantises need defining at this point.

I added a bit of suggested definition on the flowers, a bit more foliage in the back, and both mantises now have faces, and they are looking at you! I could have, and maybe should have, stopped here.

However, I decided to add darker grey-green leaves because the mantises wanted more leaves to hide in. Notice how everything changes your perception of the painting when the background is darker. Most paintings are not masterpieces, but personal treasures. I encourage you to paint from your heart; paint something that touches you.

OIL PAINTING — FOCUS ON DESIGN

Oil Painting Supplies: For the most part, I use the same supplies in the studio as I do painting outside in the field.
- Limited Palette: There are many variations, and I change paints, but here are the basics: Cadmium Red, French Ultramarine Blue, Cadmium Yellow Light, Yellow Ochre, Titanium White, Alizarin Crimson, Dioxazine Purple, Raw Sienna, and Raw Umber.
- Gamblin Artist's Oil Colors
- Gamsol solvent with Neo Megilp medium most of the time
- Easel
- Solvent bucket (seen hanging from my easel in the photo)
- A variety of oil painting long-handled brushes
- Towels/rags

June Fireflies, Falls Church, oil on panel 16 in. x 20 in.

One warm June evening, I set up to paint the fireflies in my yard. As the sun began to set, I tried to establish my composition using my usual limited palette. This was helpful because it was getting dark, and I always put my colors in the same place on the palette. I do the same with my gouache palette. The focus of this painting was to be the fireflies as they emerged with the diminishing light; hence, the basic painting needed to be dark with a variety of interest within the dark composition and no confusing lights. I live inside the Washington, D.C. beltway; it never really gets utterly dark like it does in June Lake, CA. My yard has many trees, so the fireflies are at home here. They live in the dried leaves on the ground left from winter. Another excuse not to rake!

I covered my palette with parchment paper, rather than using the wood palette so I could see better. The arrangement of colors on the palette is my usual configuration.

June Fireflies, Falls Church, oil on panel 16 in. x 20 in.

Snow path to the My Studio, Falls Church, oil on panel 8 in. x 11 in.

Here in the Washington, D.C. area, we are held hostage by the snow when it comes in abundance. This usually occurs about every 7 years, and I generally am delighted to paint from a window. This composition has a stripe of detail, a wedge of blue shadowed snow, and a larger wedge of sunlit snow.

ADVANTAGES OF OIL PAINT AND THE STUDIO

I spend time painting in the field learning about the light and weather and how the leaves turn and shimmer when a storm is near. However, I also spend time in my studio, working large and tacking linen canvas on the wall to begin a painting. I start by sorting out the elements for design.

Constitution Garden, Virginia,
oil on linen 72 in. x 55 in.

I began this as a commission painting for a large, lush garden, and Virginia is the place to find these. Everything grows here, and fast, but by mid-summer the greens take over.

We visited Montpelier, James and Dollie Madison's home, where the Virginia Garden Society maintains a beautiful garden However, even an organized garden doesn't make for a great painting. It needs to be orchestrated. Taking bits and pieces from what was there, I began to paint.

The wall and tree provided structure and earth tones. I cut the wall off and added the path, so the viewer wasn't trapped by the wall. This is day two of work with large brushes organizing the space. I had taken many photos of the area to use as a reference while painting. As I went further into the painting design, I selected foliage of different colors and large different shaped leaves to help vary the composition.

It is essential to work all over the space right from the beginning, as fast as you can. Avoid all detail and think only about the design.

Writing teachers tell students to write their essays without stopping to correct grammar or spelling, to quickly get their thoughts on paper. This is what we are doing here, getting our thoughts onto the canvas no matter how messy it looks. This is an underpainting.

Using the concepts of creating deep space on a flat plane. I started to bring in my darkest darks for the foreground.

When dealing with deep space, your darkest darks. lightest lights, and the greatest amount of detail are in the foreground. This all diminishes as you move back into the distance. When you reach the distant space. colors, or values are in the light- to mid-range with no detail.

I finished covering the canvas with the underpainting and cropped the size to check the composition.

At this point, I realized I needed a visual reminder of where the edge of the painting was to be after the canvas was stretched around a stretcher, so I added the tape.

This demo is focused on design and composition; notice how important establishing the edges are to the design. On most smaller paintings, the canvas is stretched when I start; however, working flat on the wall creates a better gallery-wrapped edge for unframed paintings. Beginning a more in-depth detailed process, the painting moves along much slower. It is important to continue to work on areas all over the canvas bringing it to a mid-stage of development.

This flowering perennial hibiscus wasn't growing there; I positioned it in the painting as an element of design making sure the light filtering in from the sun matched the rest of the painting. Oil painting allows for as many additions as you wish to consider. It is by far the most flexible, durable, and beautiful of the mediums, but more complex while painting.

Now it is time to stretch the canvas on heavy-duty wooden stretchers, and add my favorite things. All of my paintings are personal, and this little dark-eyed junco visits my bird feeder all through the winter months and retreats to the mountains as the weather warms, so I followed it to the hills around Montpelier as I was painting.

This lady cardinal is a year-round backyard pal and wanted to pose for the painting. These are my last additions to the garden painting.

Constitution Garden, Virginia, Oil on linen 72 in. x 55 in.

Following the Colorado River, Utah, oil on panel 10 in. x 10 in.

Design is about percentages of the canvas in color, form, and space.

Following the Colorado River, Utah II, oil on panel 10 in. x 10 in.

Please join me at my website **www.alexiascott.com**, where you will find stories about my paintings, learn about new work, and subscribe to my monthly newsletter, Fine Art News. The newsletter gives you painting ideas and tips, and you can even ask me questions about painting nature. I hope you will feel inspired to paint and enjoy the nature around you. It is not necessary to travel far from home to find nature to paint.

Pop Quiz: Look through my images. Try to decide which of the 5 elements of art and design were primary and then secondary while I was painting. The more you study the picture plane, the easer natural design will become for you and your painting process.

"In any moment of decision, the best thing you can do is the right thing, the next best thing is the wrong thing, and the worst thing you can do is nothing."

—TEDDY ROOSEVELT,
FRIEND OF THE NATIONAL PARKS

Left Image: Sitting in the Field near Bull Run , Virginia, **oil on linen 22 in. x 30 in.**

Left Image: Fall Leaves and Branches, Virginia, oil on linen 22 in. x 30 in.

Made in the USA
Middletown, DE
20 October 2021

50644963R00042